Dear Friends,

When it comes to couture for dolls, Susan York has a wonderful ability to weave magic with cloth, creating beautiful heirloom garments that would make even the plainest of dolls appear radiant.

Hailing from Nashville, Tennessee in the US, Susan has been designing her exquisite dolls' outfits for many years, having started out as a sewer of children's clothing. Her work incorporates beautiful fabrics, interesting techniques and delicate trimmings, all with a distinctive Victorian influence.

Susan shares 10 of her beautiful designs with comprehensive instructions and helpful advice all along the way. You will soon discover that Susan loves to create her garments with a theme, whether it be a new frock for the first day of school, something to snuggle into at a slumber party, a colourful outfit for an Easter parade, an elegant dress for a tea party or a fairytale gown fit for a princess. Your dolls are in for a real treat!

You will find some of the garments are relatively simple to sew, while others involve more complex techniques. You can either sew the clothing just as you see it or, even better, use the pictures as inspiration to create your own masterpieces.

Even if you are not a sewer, you can still enjoy seeing the colourful photographs and enchanting stories that accompany each project. We also have an interesting chat with Susan and find out a little more about her background and learn the secret behind her success.

I hope you all have hours and hours of fun with this magazine, it certainly has been a joy putting it all together.

Happy Stitching,

EDITOR

Dressing Dolls

with Susan York

GUEST EDITOR Gloria McKinnon
SERIES EDITOR Kirsty Holmes
PROJECT COORDINATOR Margaret Taylor
PHOTOGRAPHER Chris Patterson
STYLISTS Fay King, Gloria McKinnon
GRAPHIC DESIGN Annette Tamone
ILLUSTRATION Lesley Griffith
PHOTOGRAPHIC DIRECTOR
Robyn Wilson
EDITORIAL COORDINATOR
Chris Hietbrink
PUBLISHER Sue Aiken

PUBLISHED BY
Express Publications Pty Ltd
ACN 057 807 904 under licence from
EP Investments Pty Ltd ACN 003 109 055
(1995)

2 Stanley Street, Silverwater NSW 2128
Tel: (02) 9748 0599 Fax: (02) 9748 1956

PRINTED BY
Times Printers Pte Ltd, Singapore

Quilter's Resource ISBN 1-889682-09-8
This edition first published in 1999 for
Quilters' Resource Inc
PO Box 148850
Chicago, IL 60614
Tel: 773 278-5695

Contents

Easter Parade

Chocolate and sugar eggs displayed in shop windows announce that Easter is close at hand and with it comes the excitement of dressing up in new Easter frocks and bonnets. This traditional outfit features lots of lace insertion, puffing, frills and ribbons for that olde worlde look.

MATERIALS

- 1m (1 1/8yd) Swiss Nelona or batiste
- 6m x 13mm (6 5/8yd x 1/2in) cotton edging lace
- 1.5m x 35mm (1 5/8yd x 1 3/8in) cotton lace edging for bonnet
- 2m x 9mm (2 1/4yd x 3/8in) cotton insertion lace
- 2m x 13mm (2 1/4yd x 1/2in) cotton insertion lace
- 1m (1 1/8yd) fine entredeux
- 3/4m (7/8yd) narrow beading
- 1.5m x 4mm (1 2/3yd x 1/8in) double-sided satin ribbon
- 1.2m x 2.5cm (1 2/3yd x 1in) double-sided satin ribbon for ties on bonnet
- 28cm x 6mm (1/3yd x 1/4in) elastic
- Skein each of pale green and lemon embroidery cotton
- Two 6mm (1/4in) buttons
- Matching sewing threads
- Needle for embroidery
- Water-soluble fabric marker
- Usual sewing requirements including duckbill scissors and bodkin

To fit doll:
46cm (18in)
Finished length of dress:
32cm (12 1/2in)

PREPARATION

Trace the pattern pieces from the pattern sheets, transferring all markings. A 6mm (1/4in) seam allowance is included in the pattern. Read instructions carefully before cutting your fabric.

DRESS

Working on the T-front piece first, fold in half lengthwise and lightly press so you will have a visual point to work from to position the lace insertions. The T is made a little long to make sure it will match up with the side skirts and can be trimmed later.

Cut the four pieces of the smaller insertion lace 12.5cm (approx 5in) long and fold in half, right sides together. Position the lace over the placement guide on the pattern with the bottom of the fold on the bottom of the V. The centre line on the pattern shows you where the stitching line must be. Mark and pin, then stitch using a small zigzag stitch and trim away the excess lace. Press flat.

Position lace onto T-panel using water-soluble fabric marker to mark placement lines and pin to hold. Attach lace along heading with a zigzag stitch wide enough to cover all of the heading. Very carefully cut the fabric away from the back of the lace using duckbill scissors.

Cut two more pieces of the smaller insertion lace 26cm (10 1/4in) long and position each side of the T as shown on the pattern. Pin in place and mitre the corner and zigzag as before. Cut fabric away from behind the lace.

Cut two side skirts 17.8cm x 21.5cm (7in x 8 1/2in). Using the armhole guide on the pattern sheet, cut out the armhole from the shorter ends of fabric, making sure you have a pair. Gather the top of each panel to fit the T-yoke and pin. Zigzag side pieces to the insertion lace, then trim fabric out from behind.

In the same way attach the smaller lace insertion to the back yokes, extending lace 2.5cm (1in) past the fold line. Trim excess fabric from behind, and fold under the extra lace tail, zigzag through the lace 1.3cm ($^{1}/_{2}$in) from the edge and trim away any extra lace.

Cut the back skirt panel 21.5cm x 56cm wide (8$^{1}/_{2}$in x 22in). Slash down centre 7.5cm (3in) from the top and attach a lace placket as instructed for the petticoat in the White Christmas ensemble, using the smaller insertion lace. Cut out armhole curves using the guide on the pattern sheet. Run two rows of gathering thread to fit back yokes. Attach to lace insertion with a fine zigzag stitch and trim away excess fabric from behind.

French seam front and back shoulder seams together. To make a very fine seam, stitch with wrong sides together, using a small zigzag stitch so that the needle falls off the edge of the fabric causing it to roll. Press flat, then stitch again with right sides together, just enclosing the roll.

Sleeves: Gather bottom of sleeve edge to 14cm (5$^{1}/_{2}$in) and attach entredeux, beading, and gathered lace edging with a fine zigzag stitch.

With two rows of gathering threads, gather top of sleeve to fit armhole. Stitch into place and neaten edges.

Using a French seam, join one skirt side and sleeve seam in a line starting at the lace edge of the sleeve.

Cut a strip of the wider insertion lace to fit the hem of the dress and attach with a zigzag stitch.

Cut and French seam pieces of fabric to measure 5cm x 2.3m (2in x 2$^{1}/_{2}$yd) for the puffing. Run two rows of gathering threads on both sides, then gather to fit bottom edge of dress. Zigzag puffing onto lace insertion, covering lace heading and inner row of gathering thread of puffing. Trim excess fabric. Place another row of insertion lace below the puffing and attach with a zigzag stitch. Trim.

French seam strips of fabric to measure a piece 7.6cm x 2.3m (3in x 2$^{1}/_{2}$yd) for the ruffle. Attach narrow lace edging to one side, then trim away excess fabric.

Gather ruffle to fit bottom edge of dress. Zigzag to lace insertion joining lace heading to inner row of gathering thread on ruffle. Trim excess fabric.

French seam the other side seam, catching in all the ends of the skirt trimmings.

To finish neck edge, attach entredeux and gathered lace edging, extending past the neck edge 2.5cm (1in). Fold lace ends under, even with the yoke and zigzag on the fold, then trim.

Add a 6mm ($^{1}/_{4}$in) button to the back yoke and run the 4mm ($^{1}/_{8}$in) ribbon through the beading on the sleeves.

Embroider a pretty trim of pale green feather stitch leaves and French knot flowers at the centre front yoke and around the skirt.

BONNET

Cut a piece of fabric 5cm x 114.5cm (2in x 1$^{1}/_{4}$yd) for the ruffle. Attach lace edging to one side, then trim.

Using a zigzag stitch, attach the smaller insertion lace around the band following the pattern guide. Mitre the corners and join the ends. Then trim fabric from behind.

Run two rows of gathering thread across the top of bonnet crown as indicated on pattern and gather to fit the band. Place in position against

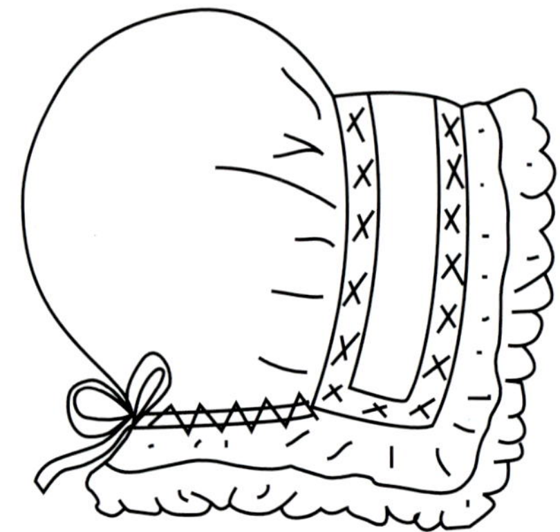

the lace insertion on the band. Zigzag to the inner gathering thread of the bonnet, then trim fabric.

Join ends of ruffle with a fine French seam. Run two rows of gathering threads on the long side of the ruffle. Mark the centre and match to the centre of the band. Gather ruffle to fit all way around the bonnet. Zigzag ruffle to lace insertion, stitching on inner row of gathering threads of ruffle. On the back of the bonnet where there is no lace insertion, flip up the ruffle so that right sides are together and join with a normal seam. Trim and neaten edges.

Cut two pieces of 4mm (1/8in) ribbon 30.5cm (12in) long. Position over ruffle seam across back of bonnet and secure ends of ribbon at the sides. Zigzag a casing over the ribbon. Draw up back bonnet with the ribbon and tie a bow.

If you wish, add another ruffle of the wide lace edging around the headband, as on our bonnet. Join to the outside edge of the insertion lace with a fine zigzag.

Cut two pieces of the wide ribbon 46cm (approx 18in) long. Attach to the inside of the front headband, folding the raw ends under.

PETTICOAT

To make the petticoat with pintucks, cut a square of fabric 28cm (11in). Sew 11 pintucks 7.5cm (3in) long at the centre of one side, spacing them to fit the neckline of the petticoat front, as our garment shows.

Centre the front pattern piece over the pintucks and cut out. Make a 7.6cm (3in) long slash down centre back and attach a lace placket using the smaller insertion lace.

French seam front to back at the shoulder seam.

Position lace edging around the neckline so that the fancy edge of lace is even with the cut edge of fabric and the ends extend 2.5cm (1in) from the placket. As you get to the centre front V, position lace carefully, pin and zigzag from the back of lace forming a mitred corner. Trim away excess lace. Continue on around the neckline, fold under the tails at centre back. Zigzag close to fold and trim.

Do the same for the armholes.

French seam one side of petticoat. Zigzag a length of the wider insertion lace to the hem covering lace heading, and trim fabric.

Cut a piece of fabric 7.6cm x 114.5cm (3in x 45in) for the ruffle, zigzag lace edging to the bottom and trim. Run two rows of gathering thread to the top of the ruffle and gather to fit bottom of petticoat. Position ruffle to the edge of insertion lace and stitch along inner row of gathering threads, using a zigzag stitch. Trim away excess fabric from underneath the lace.

Sew the other side of petticoat with a French seam. Add button or press stud for the back closure.

PANTALOONS

French seam the centre front crotch seam. Narrow hem the top edge of the pantaloons and fold under a 1.3cm (1/2in) casing and stitch close to the edge. Run a 28cm (11in) piece of 6mm (1/4in) wide elastic through the casing and secure ends. Stitch down elastic through the casing at several points to prevent elastic from twisting.

Stitch the centre back with a small French seam.

Gather bottom of legs to 15.2cm (6in) and attach entredeux, beading and gathered lace edging.

With right sides together, stitch inside leg seams, matching crotch seams. Trim raw edges and neaten.

Run the 4mm (1/4in) ribbon through the beading and leave enough tail to tie a bow.♥

Tea by the Sea

Plan a Tea by the Sea tea party to bring to life one of those Victorian seaside holidays often depicted in 19th century illustrations. Be prepared for sun, sand and sea in these charming party pants featuring a very old technique with a fresh new look.

MATERIALS

- 40cm (1/2yd) cotton fabric with 6mm (1/4in) alternating stripe
- 25cm (1/4yd) plain cotton fabric
- 2m (2 1/4yd) rickrack
- Water-soluble marking pen
- 20cm (8in) Wonder-Under fusible webbing
- 3 x 10mm (1/2in) buttons
- 60cm x 3mm (24in x 1/8in) elastic
- Matching sewing threads
- Usual sewing requirements

To fit doll:
40.5cm (16in)
Finished length of outfit:
28cm (11in)

PREPARATION

Trace the patterns from the pattern sheet and transfer all relevant markings. Back bodices are cut on the fold but are treated as a single layer. A 6mm (1/4in) seam allowance is included. You will need to pre-tuck the fabric before cutting the front bodice. By using a striped fabric for this technique, much of the work is out of the way because you don't have to draw lots of horizontal lines. For the design shown, four rows of horizontal stripes make a 1.3cm (1/2in) tuck. If you want a finer tuck, use only 2 rows of stripes per tuck, making a 6mm (1/4in) tuck.

BODICE

The front of the bodice starts with a block approximately 28cm x 38cm (11in x 15in). Count up from either the bottom or the top, six rows, and fold on that striped line between the two colours. Pin the fold across. With a short straight stitch length

(1.5 to 2.0) stitch a tuck on the second stripe from the fold. Continue in the same way until you have eight tucks, with the four stripes at the top and the bottom remaining.

Now transfer the pyramid pattern to your tucked bodice block. Measure and find the centre of the piece and mark with a water-soluble marker. Start on the bottom row and draw the eight marks which will form seven little sharks teeth. Repeat for the remaining rows until all eight rows have been marked. Cut eight strips of Wonder-Under the width of the block.Trim strips to 1.3cm (½in) wide approximately, saving the 6mm (¼in) piece for another project.

Iron the Wonder-Under to the wrong side of the tucks, only

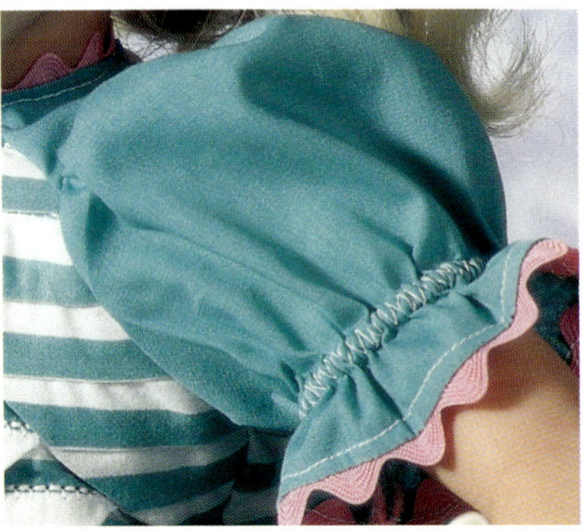

removing the paper when you are ready to fold the sharks teeth. Starting at the bottom tuck, peel the paper away and carefully snip to the stitching, but not through it, on the pyramid lines you have drawn.

Beginning on the bottom row, fold the cut edges of the clipped tuck under so that the point of the fold just covers the stitching line of the tuck. Repeat for all tucks and as you finish each row, starch and press tucks into points. To finish, change your machine needle to a 100 to 110 size denim or top stitch needle. Set your machine for a pin-stitch program, length 3.0 and width 2.0. Pin stitch the top of each tuck line to hold the points firmly in position.

Centre the front bodice pattern piece over block of tucked fabric and cut out. Try to match stripes at side seams when you cut out the back bodice. Stitch shoulder yokes to front and back bodice and neaten the edges.

SLEEVES

Run two rows of gathering thread across the top of the sleeve and gather

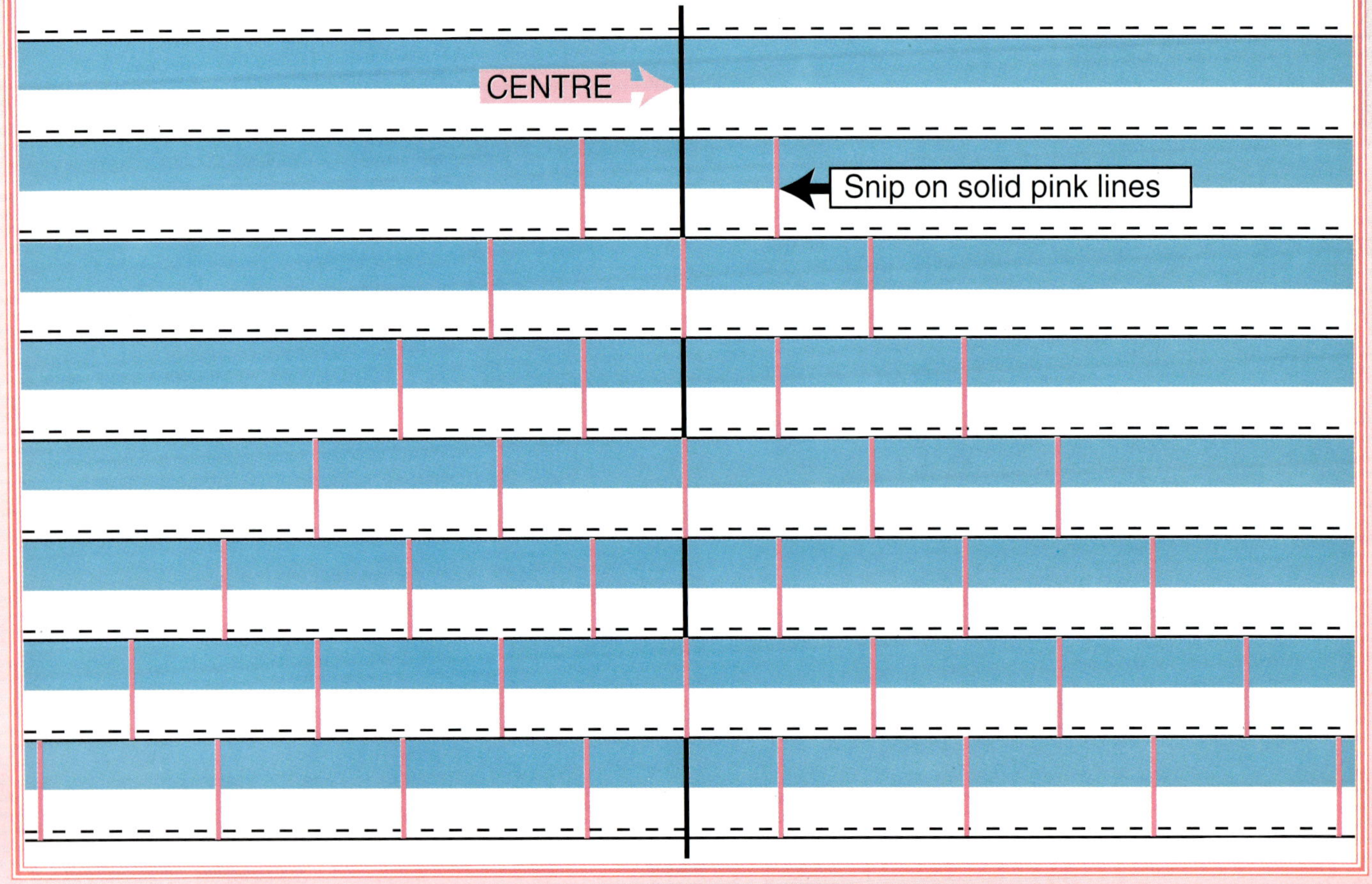

CENTRE

Snip on solid pink lines

to fit armhole, matching the little hearts. Then stitch and neaten edges.

Narrow hem the bottom of sleeve edge or finish with rickrack trim. If using rickrack, position trim on top of the right side of sleeve, at the raw edge, and straight stitch through the centre of trim. Fold trim on stitching line to the wrong side and top stitch close to the fold line. Only half the scallop of the trim will show.

Zigzag 3mm (1/8in) elastic to the wrong side of sleeve where indicated on the pattern. Pull elastic to 11.5cm (4 1/2in) and secure ends.

Cut a strip of fabric 7.6cm x 114.5cm (3in x 45in) for the sash; cut into two pieces, decorate one end of each with rickrack as on the sleeves, and narrow hem the sides. Gather the raw ends to 2.5cm (1in) and position on the back bodice, right sides up, just above the second stripe and pin. With right sides together, stitch bodice sleeve and side seams catching in the sashes. Finish the neck edge with a bias strip or rickrack trim as you did for the sleeves.

PANTS

Sew centre front and centre back seams, trim and neaten. Slash down 7.5cm (3in) on centre back seamline and insert a continuous placket using a bias strip of fabric and press.

Run two rows of gathering threads across the top edge of pants and gather to fit bodice. Stitch with right sides together, matching centre backs, using a 1.5cm (1/2in) seam. You can use the stripes as a guide and be careful not to catch the points of the tucks in the seam. Trim and neaten edges.

Narrow hem the bottom edge of pants or use rickrack as on the sleeves. Attach 3mm (1/8in) elastic where indicated on the pattern. Turn to wrong side and sew the inside leg seam, matching crotch seams. Trim and neaten.

Finish off neck edge with bias fabric strip or rickrack and add three buttons to the back bodice.♥

School Days

Cooler weather is on the way and these delightful party pants from the School Days series will be perfect for that most important first day back at school.

PREPARATION

Transfer the pattern pieces from the pattern sheet, copying all markings. A 6mm (1/4in) seam allowance has been included. Read the instructions carefully before cutting your fabric. In the outfit pictured, contrasting fabrics have been used to great effect for the bodice, sleeves and sash, with matching decorative stitching and buttons.

COLLAR

The top collar is embellished with satin stitching of different widths. Use a layer of tear-away stabiliser under the fabric to stitch the design. Transfer the decorative stitching line to the collar, using a transfer pen. You simply trace the pattern onto tracing paper using the pen, position face down on fabric, press and the motif is transferred. Set your machine for a width of 3.0 and a length of 0.25 and stitch line No1, then set your machine to a width of 2.5 and a length of 0.25 to stitch line No 2. Press and tear away stabiliser.

Sew lining to collar with right sides together around the outer edge. Clip corners, trim, turn and press. Set aside.

MATERIALS

- 30cm (3/8yd) plain medium weight fabric
- 20cm (1/4yd) plaid medium weight fabric
- Three 15mm (5/8in) buttons
- Machine embroidery thread
- Matching sewing thread
- Tear-away stabiliser
- Transfer pen
- Tracing paper
- Usual sewing requirements

To fit doll:
46cm (18in)
Finished length of outfit:
39cm (15 1/2in)

BODICE

The front bodice pieces are cut on the fold to form a double layer but are treated as a single layer. Sew front and back bodices together at shoulder seams and set aside.

Stitch a box pleat in bottom of sleeve as indicated on pattern and press. Refer to Diagram 1. Fold cuff in half lengthwise, wrong sides together and gather bottom of sleeve to fit. With right sides together, stitch cuff to sleeve and neaten edges. Press.

Run two rows of gathering threads across top of sleeve and gather to fit armhole and stitch.

Diagram 1

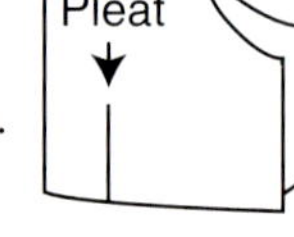

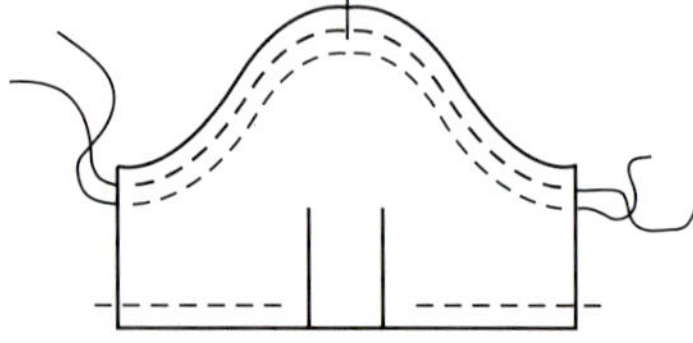

Cut sash strip 7.5cm x 1.15m (3in x 1 1/4yd). Narrow hem long sides, fold in half and stitch ends, then press sash flat. The ends will form a neat point. Cut in half to give two sashes 57cm (22in) long. Gather raw ends to 2.5cm (1in) and stitch between front waistband pieces as indicated on pattern and stitch. Refer to Diagram 2.

Stitch front waistband to front bodice pieces with right sides together and do the same with back waistband and bodice.

With right sides together, sew front and back bodice together at side and underarm seams.

Cut a 2.5cm x 25cm (1in x 1/4yd)

4
2
6
READING

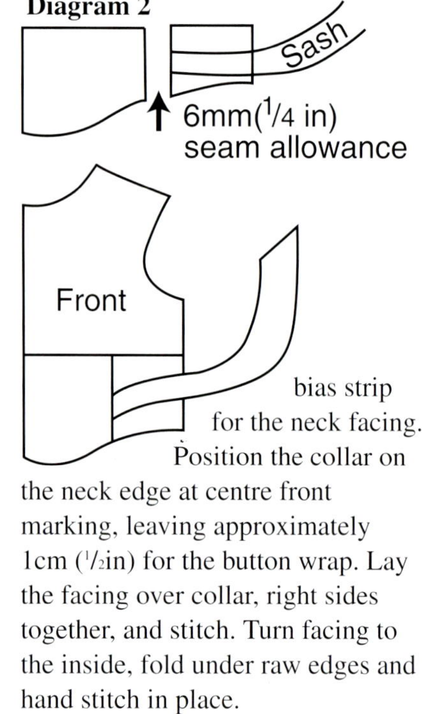

bias strip for the neck facing. Position the collar on the neck edge at centre front marking, leaving approximately 1cm (1/2in) for the button wrap. Lay the facing over collar, right sides together, and stitch. Turn facing to the inside, fold under raw edges and hand stitch in place.

PANTS

Stitch centre front and back seams. Trim centre front seam to 3mm (1/8in) and neaten edges. Measure down 7.6cm (3in) on centre front seam and slash on stitching line. Make placket using a bias strip of fabric or grosgrain ribbon.

Gather the bottom of the leg edge to fit cuff. Fold cuff in half lengthwise, wrong sides together. Match raw edges of cuff and pants and stitch, right sides together. Trim and neaten edges. Stitch inside leg seams, matching crotch seams.

Run two rows of gathering threads to top of pants and gather to fit the waistband. Match centre front edges and side notches of pants to side bodice seam. With right sides together, stitch pants to waistband and neaten.

Add the three buttons and buttonholes to the front to finish.♥

SPECIAL OFFER

Quilters' Resource Inc is proud to introduce you to the superb *Australian Dolls, Bears and Collectables* and *Bear Creations* magazines. If you are enjoying this book, *Dressing Dolls with Susan York*, then you'll simply adore both *Australian Dolls, Bears and Collectables* and *Bear Creations*. Each of these stunning magazines is designed to inspire and challenge all crafters, from beginners to advanced.

SUBSCRIBE NOW AND SAVE UP TO $25.00!

AUSTRALIAN DOLLS, BEARS AND COLLECTABLES $6.95

Every time you open the breathtaking *Australian Dolls, Bears and Collectables* magazine, you enter a magical world brimming with authoritative features, informative news, exciting how-to projects and beautiful photography.

Bear Creations features at least four enchanting teddy patterns in each vibrant issue. There's also a wealth of bear-themed projects to keep you busy, using folk art, quilting, cross stitch and a variety of other crafts.

BEAR CREATIONS $6.95

EACH MAGAZINE HAS:

- a double-sided tear-out pattern sheet
- full-color photographs
- clear, step-by-step instructions
- more than 80 pages of projects and information

SUBSCRIPTION ORDER FORM

YES! Please enter my subscription/s to the magazine series below:

☐ 8 issues of *Australian Dolls, Bears and Collectables* for $46.50
☐ 8 issues of *Bear Creations* for $46.50
Each subscription includes the special annual issue priced at $7.95.
SAVE OVER $10.00!
Add $10.00 for Canadian and other Foreign Subscriptions.

☐ 16 issues of *Australian Dolls, Bears and Collectables* for $87.75
☐ 16 issues of *Bear Creations* for $87.75
Each subscription includes two special annual issues priced at $7.95 each.
SAVE OVER $25.00!
Add $20.00 for Canadian and other Foreign Subscriptions.

HOW TO ORDER

Mail to: Quilters' Resource Inc,
PO Box 148850
CHICAGO, IL 60614

FAX US AT: **1-800-216-2374**
OR: **1-773-278-1348**

Name: ______________________
Address: ______________________
City, State/Province/County: ______________________
Zip Code: __________ Tel. No: (____) ______________
PAYMENT DETAILS I enclose a check in U.S. funds payable to **Quilters' Resource Inc** for US $__________
OR charge my ○ Visa ○ Mastercard for $ ________
Credit Card No: ☐☐☐☐☐☐☐☐☐☐☐☐☐☐☐☐
Expiry Date: ____ / ____ Signature: ______________________

Cinderella

As in all good fairytales, all ends happily ever after as Cinderella marries her Prince. And doesn't she look enchanting! In majestic white organza and lace, she'll sweep him off his royal feet.

MATERIALS

- 80cm (7/8yd) Spark organza
- 20cm (1/4yd) satin for bodice
- 7m x 6mm (7 5/8yd x 1/4in) white double-sided satin ribbon
- 80cm (7/8yd) all-over lace net
- 50cm (1/2yd) tulle
- 20cm x 10mm (1/4yd x 1/2in) cotton lace edging
- 30cm x 10mm (3/8yd x 1/2in) elastic
- Three pearl buttons
- 20cm (1/4yd) string of decorative pearls
- Small gold heart charm
- Hair clip to attach veil
- Hot glue gun or similar
- White sewing thread
- Stiff interfacing or cardboard for tiara
- Sequins or glitter for tiara
- Usual sewing requirements

To fit doll:
46cm (18in)
Finished length of dress:
39cm (15 1/2in)

PREPARATION

Trace the pattern from the pattern sheets noting all markings. There is a 6mm (1/4in) seam allowance unless otherwise instructed. Read the instructions carefully before cutting your fabric.

DRESS

Skirt: Cut fabric for the skirt tiers to the following measurements: Top tier 11.4cm x 114.5cm (4 1/2in x 45in); middle tier 21.5cm x 114.5cm (8 1/2in x 45in); bottom tier 32cm x 114.5cm (12 1/2in x 45in).

Satin ribbon trims the scalloped skirt edges.

The lace sleeves feature a 'leg o' mutton' treatment.

Work on each skirt tier separately. Transfer the scallop design from the pattern sheets to the bottom of each tier, 1.3cm (1/2in) from the raw edge. On the top and middle tiers the trim continues up the back of the skirt with trimmed edges slightly overlapping. The bottom tier is joined by a centre back seam. The scallops and trim are taken across the bottom only.

Use the 6mm (1/4in) double-sided satin ribbon to finish off the scallops. Working at the ironing board you can curve the ribbon into the scallop shape, pinning each scallop and across the mitred points as you go.

Attach ribbon with a small zigzag stitch on the inside curve of the design. Carefully trim away extra fabric from behind ribbon.

Stitch the centre back seam on the bottom tier and trim raw edges. Cut down approximately 9cm (3 1/2in) on the stitching line from the top and attach a lace placket.

To do the placket, cut a piece of insertion lace approx 20.5cm (8in) long. Pull fabric so it forms a V shape and position the lace to the V with right sides together. Allow 3mm (1/8in) of fabric to extend past the lace.

Using a small, close zigzag stitch, sew lace to fabric. Press the right side of the placket under and the left side will extend over the fabric. On the inside, zigzag down a dart in the lace at the fold of the V and trim away excess lace. Press.

Bodice: Stitch the shoulder seams. Position the satin ribbon in the criss-cross design following the motif in the pattern sheet.

Two lengths of ribbon are stitched either side of the motif to secure. These ribbons extend from the front waist to the back waist over the shoulders. Stitch either side of the border ribbons with a small zigzag stitch.

Cut a piece of fabric 7.5cm x 1.14m (3in x 44in) for the sash and cut in half to give two 57cm (22in) long pieces. Narrow hem sides and finish ends by stitching with right sides together. Turn and press flat and you have a neat pointed end. Gather other end to 2.5cm (1in) and position right side up on back bodice, 1.3cm (1/2in) up from waist. Set aside.

Finish neck edge with a narrow bias band 2.5cm (1in) wide. Stitch with right sides together. Turn in the ends, then fold band to the inside and hand stitch in place. Hand stitch the decorative pearls to the neckline with the small gold heart at centre front.

Sleeves: Gather bottom edge of top sleeve piece to fit the top of straight sleeve piece. Stitch, then trim edges. Narrow hem the bottom edge of sleeve. Run two rows of gathering threads across top of sleeve and gather to fit bodice armhole. Stitch and trim edges.

With bodice folded right sides together, stitch the sleeve and side seams, using a small zigzag stitch to join the lace sections. Catch the ends of sash in the seamline. Neaten the edges and then set aside.

Gather each tier of the skirt to fit the bodice and attach, starting with the top tier. Match the ends of the ribbon trim to the edge of bodice backs. Trim and neaten edges.

Finish off the dress with the three pearl buttons on the back bodice.

TIARA

You can make the tiara by cutting out the pattern from interfacing or cardboard, covering it with glue, then sprinkling it with glitter or sequins. Attach to the hairclip, under the veil, with hot glue.

VEIL

Cut veil 30.5cm x 56cm (12in x 22in) and round off the edges using the guide. Stitch the 6mm (1/4in) double-sided satin ribbon around three sides, with a fine zigzag stitch. Gather the top edge of the veil to fit the hairclip and hot-glue in place.

Make a fabric bow with a 15cm x 30.5cm (6in x 12in) piece of organza. Fold in half lengthwise and stitch. Trim and neaten edges. Turn tube to right side, sew raw ends together, then tie a small piece of satin ribbon around the centre to make a bow. Hot-glue in place to cover raw edges of the veil.

CRINOLINE

Fold the length of tulle in half lengthwise and pin. Fold a rectangle lengthwise from the remainder of the lace and fold over the tulle layer. It doesn't matter if the lace is shorter than the tulle layer as this will help the crinoline to stand out. Stitch a 1.6cm (5/8in) casing on the fold line to make a skirt length of 24cm (1/4yd). Run the elastic through and secure. Stitch through the casing and the elastic in several places to prevent the elastic from twisting. Stitch the centre back seam and neaten. ♥

Ribbons, pearls and a heart charm decorate the bodice.

The veil and tiara are attached to the hairclip at the back.

Mystery Tea

An anonymous letter arrives in the mail with an invitation to a Mystery Tea. Sounds intriguing, but what to wear? Time to get creative and learn this old technique of Celtic appliqué and contemporary machine Battenburg embroidery to decorate a charming flannel frock.

MATERIALS

- 40cm (1/2yd) mediumweight plaid
- 50cm (2/3yd) plain brown fabric
- Scrap of black ultra-suede
- Three 10mm (1/2in) buttons
- Matching thread
- Machine embroidery cotton
- Bias bar, 7/8in for 1/4in bar
- Transfer pen
- Tracing paper
- Water-soluble glue
- Vanish-A-Way stabiliser
- Bow whip
- Usual sewing requirements

To fit doll:
46cm (18in)
Finished length of dress:
26cm (10 1/4in)

PREPARATION

Trace the pattern from the pattern sheet and transfer all markings. A 6mm (1/4in) seam allowance is included. Cut a piece of fabric for the skirt 30.5cm x 115cm (12in x 45in).

SKIRT

Cut several bias strips from the plain fabric 2.5cm (1in) wide, leaving a 10cm-wide piece for the sash. If your machine has a 6mm (1/4 in) quilting foot attachment, use it to sew your

bias strips as exact measurements are most crucial.

Fold your bias strips in half lengthwise, wrong sides together, and sew a 6mm (1/4in) seam, keeping seam as straight as possible. Sew only about 33cm (12in) and then check that the bias bar will slip through the tube; if not, adjust your seam allowance. If it slips through easily, finish sewing the remainder of the bias.

Trim the seam, being careful not to cut the stitching. Do not turn the tube. Insert the bias bar into the tube and press lightly, without steam, slipping the bar along the tube as you press. Make sure that the raw edges and the stitching are on the back. Be careful as this bar can get very hot.

After you have pressed with the bias bar, press again without it. Finally, press from the right side to make the folds smooth and crisp. It is not recommended that you use continuous bias as the bias bar usually gets caught in the seams. If you do choose to use continuous bias, press all the seams in one direction and make sure the bias bar is moved in the same direction as the seams are pressed.

Fold up a 7.6cm (3in) hem to the wrong side of the skirt, then fold raw edge under 6mm (1/4in). Using the transfer pen, trace single lines of the skirt motif shown on the pattern sheet onto tracing paper.

Lay the transfer sheet face down on the right side of the fabric and press. The lines of the motif will be transferred to the fabric. Depending upon the fabric, you may be able to use the same transfer several times before having to re-trace the lines on the pattern.

Position the motif 6.4cm (2 1/2in) up from the fold of the hem as indicated on the guide. Transfer the motif 6mm (1/4in) from the selvedge of the fabric, and continue across the skirt until you reach the other side. You will have to decide where the pattern repeat stops in order to match the pattern at the back seam. You may end up with fabric left at one end, which can be trimmed. There should be five complete pattern repeats.

Glue the prepared bias strips into position on the skirt following the lines of the motif, alternating the overs and unders as you go. You may need to pin the bias in place until you stitch. Make sure you tuck in as many ends as possible under another piece of bias to give a smoother look to the finished piece.

When you begin a strip, place it in the area where another strip will cover it. You may wish to cut the end at an angle in order to fit under the next strip and it may be advisable to use Fray Stop on the cut ends of the bias strips.

Once placed into position, start to stitch the bias onto the skirt using a hem stitch, just catching the edge of the bias. As you sew, your skirt will be automatically hemmed as well. Begin by sewing the outside edge of the curves first, then the tighter inside edge of the curve virtually looks after itself. To turn the corners, stitch down the outside edge, then pleat the excess material underneath and it will be caught in when you stitch the inside curves.

Leave the ends of the motif free so when the back seam is stitched, you can join the bias neatly. Stitch centre back seam, leaving a 6.5cm (2 1/2in) opening at the top for the placket. You can neaten the placket edges with some leftover bias. Trim and neaten centre back seam.

BODICE OVERLAY

To make the bias strips for the Battenburg-style overlay, cut short pieces of bias 2.5cm (1 in) wide and stitch, right sides together. Trim the seam and turn very carefully, preferably using a bow whip.

Trace bodice motif from the pattern sheet onto a layer of Vanish-A-Way, using a water-soluble marking pen. With the glue stick, glue the wrong side of the strips and position onto the stabiliser. Remember to alternate the under and overlaps.

Thread your machine top and bobbin with thread to match your fabric bias strips. Set your machine to a short straight stitch, (stitch length 1.5 to 2.0) and use your open-toe embroidery machine foot. Start with normal machine tension and straight stitch the binding down the centre, making sure the stitches catch any underlying binding strips so the design is joined together.

Place the stabiliser piece into an 18cm (7in) spring or machine embroidery hoop. Bring your bobbin thread to the top and and tie off by taking a few stitches into the very edge of one of the bias strips, wherever you plan to begin. It doesn't matter where you start. Once the threads have been tied off, you can trim them from the top and get them out of the way.

Barely catching the bias strip, straight stitch on each bridging line, reversing at the beginning and end of each line and trimming threads. Do this three or four times over each line. Re-set your machine to a zigzag stitch with a width of 1.5 and a length of 2.5 to 3.0. and zigzag over the straight stitches once. Don't forget to bring threads to the top and drag to tie off, trimming threads. This technique will form nice richelieu bars. For a heavier look, you can zigzag again over each bar.

Using a dry iron set on 'cotton', iron the Vanish-A-Way from the wrong side. The Vanish-a-Way will turn brown - don't panic, this is supposed to happen. Rub it gently between your fingers and it will fall away. You can also use an old toothbrush and gently brush to remove the Vanish-A-Way.

The piece you have just made is an overlay and is attached to the bodice at the neck and armholes.

TO SEW THE BODICE

With right sides together, stitch shoulder seams of bodice and trim.

Position the overlay onto the bodice front, pin in place and set aside.

Cut a 19cm x 2cm (7½in x ¾in) piece of ultra-suede for the stand-up collar. Stitch to neckline with right sides together, stitching through collar, overlay and bodice. You might like to cut a dip in the centre of the collar for a tailored look.

SLEEVES

Gather bottom edge of sleeve to 13cm (5¼in). Cut two strips of ultra-suede 13cm x 3.5cm (5¼in x 1½in). Stitch with right sides together.

Gather top of sleeve to fit the armhole and stitch onto bodice, catching the edges of the overlay in the seam. Trim and neaten seam.

Cut a piece of fabric 1.15m x 10cm (1¼yd x 4in) for the sash and narrow hem the long sides and cut into two pieces. Fold with right sides together and seam one end of each piece, turn and press flat. This forms a neat point on the end of sash. Gather the raw end to 1.5cm (½in) and position 1.5cm (½in) up from the waist.

Turn bodice to wrong side and stitch underarm and side seams, catching the ends of sash in the seam.

To join bodice to skirt, gather the top edge of the skirt with two rows of gathering threads to fit the bottom edge of the bodice. Stitch with right sides together matching centre backs, then neaten seam.

Finish off with the three small buttons on the bodice back.♥

Pintucks should be stitched along the straight grain of the fabric. Some sewing machines have a pintucking foot which forms the tucks automatically as you sew. Alternatively, press along the fold where you wish to place the pintuck and stitch 3mm ($^{1}/_{8}$in) in from the edge.

Sewing Techniques

These sewing techniques are used when making many of the garments presented in this issue. Thanks go to Fae Mason for demonstrating them for photography.

PINTUCKING

STRAIGHTENING THE FABRIC

For a straight edge on your fabric, always pull out a thread and cut along the line so formed.

JOINING LACES

Spray starch both pieces of lace and place them side by side so the edges are butted together but not overlapping. Machine down the join using a small zigzag just wide enough to catch the headings of both laces.

PIN STITCHING

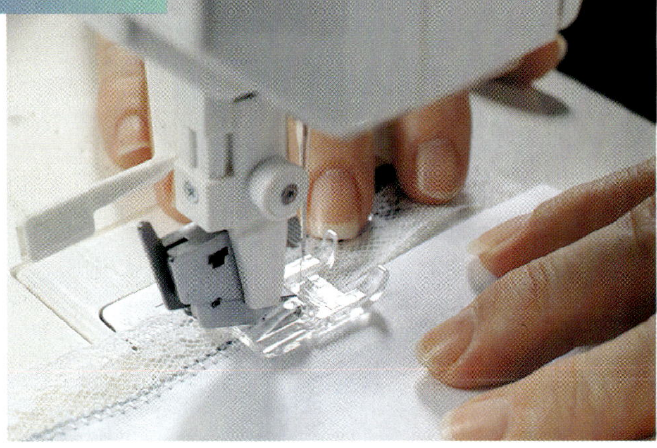

1. Pin stitching is a decorative way of attaching laces to fabric. On an Elna machine, set as above and use a 90 or 100 needle. On other machines check the respective manuals. Some machines require a wing needle.

2. Attaching the lace using pin stitching creates a decorative row of tiny holes along the edge of the fabric. Work with the fabric to your left and the lace to your right. Use either matching or contrasting thread.

PLACING GATHERING ROWS

1. When gathering fabric, stitch parallel rows of large machine stitches along the edge to be gathered.

2. Three rows of gathering stitches can allow you to pull up the fabric more evenly.

FRENCH SEAMS

1. Place the wrong sides of the two pieces of fabric together and stitch a 6mm (1/4in) seam. Carefully trim the seam allowance back to 3mm (1/8in).

2. Fold and press the fabric so the right sides are facing and stitch the seam again, enclosing the raw edges of the previous seam allowance. Press the seam to one side.

Sugar Plum Dreams

This exquisite organza gown incorporates many of the favourite techniques of heirloom sewing and will surely become a family keepsake.

MATERIALS

- 40cm ($^1/_2$yd) organza
- 30cm ($^3/_8$yd) gold lamé
- 3.5m x 20mm ($3^7/_8$yd x $^3/_4$in) cotton lace edging
- 90cm x 12mm (1yd x $^1/_2$in) lace beading
- 1m x 6mm ($1^1/_8$yd x $^1/_4$in) insertion lace – Lace A
- 4.5m x 8mm ($4^7/_8$yd x $^3/_8$in) insertion lace – Lace B
- 50cm ($^1/_2$yd) fine edging lace for petticoat neck and armholes
- 50cm ($^1/_2$yd) fine entredeux
- Four 4mm ($^1/_8$in) buttons
- 1m x 4mm ($1^1/_8$yd x $^1/_8$in) double-sided satin ribbon
- Matching sewing thread
- Water-soluble marking pen
- Usual sewing requirements including duckbill scissors and bodkin

To fit doll:
46cm (18in)
Finished length of dress:
28cm (11in)

PREPARATION

Trace pattern from the pattern sheet transferring all markings. A 6mm ($^1/_4$in) seam allowance has been included unless otherwise stated.

DRESS

Work on the teardrop panels of the skirt first, beginning with the five matching panels. Transfer the placement lines onto the panels.

Because pintucks distort the fabric, place the lace insertions on the panels first.

You will need to pull heading threads of the lace to form the curves of the design. The lace will lay flatter if you remove some of the heading threads before you gather and curve the lace. The threads you pull will be described as inside threads and the other side of the

insertion, the outside thread.

Pull about 1m (1yd) of heading thread from the wider insertion lace and adjust the gathers as you go. It will help if you press the lace as you form the design to smooth out some of the puckers. Avoid using heaving starch as this can make it difficult to pull the heading threads and they may break.

Lay the insertion as smoothly and as flat as possible. Position all three rows of insertion on the five identical panels. Stitch the inside edge of the insertion first with a zigzag stitch, covering the heading of the lace. You won't need to sew the bottom edge of the panels as they will have edging lace attached later.

Using the duckbill scissors, trim fabric from behind lace.

To make the pintucks, use a double needle size 1.6/70 or 2.0/80 and a seven groove pintuck foot. Thread your machine with two spools of thread to match your bobbin and try a sample run on a scrap of fabric. If the pintucks are puckered and too tight, loosen the top tension a little. If the tucks are not forming, you may need to tighten the top tension slightly.

Sew the pintucks following the guideline on the pattern. Position the needles in the centre of the line and use a small straight stitch. This will be the middle pintuck. For the next row, line up the first tuck in the last groove of your foot and stitch the same way. To prevent too much distortion of the fabric, alternate the sides where you start to sew on each row of tucks. Do three rows of pintucks in each section of each panel.

Rows of pin tucking and lace insertion decorate five panels of the dress.

The centre front panel features a heart motif.

Once insertions and tucks are completed, press the panels. At this stage they may not lay flat but once assembled into a dress, it will not be noticeable.

Join the five panels starting with centre back piece. Position strips of the wider insertion lace on either side of panel, leaving about 2.5cm (1in) of lace extending each end. The lace should be centred over the edge of the fabric. Attach using a zigzag stitch as before and trim fabric from behind lace.

To join the next panel, begin sewing from the bottom, matching up the lace insertions, and continue until you have joined the five panels.

The centre front panel follows the same procedure. Begin with the bottom row of insertion indicated on the pattern as lace A, then trim fabric from behind lace. Next, attach the insertion to the sides of the panel, lace B, extending the lace 2.5cm (1in) at the top and bottom as before.

Note: Where lace crosses lace, the one on top is the dominant one. Do not stitch across it. Sew only where you see the heading threads of the design and pick up the presser foot to cross over the dominant lace. Everything underneath, including other layers of lace, is cut away.

Trim fabric and lace from beneath the side insertion strips.

Use the finer insertion lace for the design at the centre of the front panel. You will need to pull the heading threads as before to curve the lace to the design. Stitch the inside thread first, then the outside, and trim fabric from behind.

Begin with the loop-heart shape and build the other laces around it. Position the lace on the design, making sure the outside threads meet at the centre of the heart shape. Mitre the point of the heart.

Sew the inside thread first remembering the rules about the dominant lace in the design.

Place the inner insertion panel of lace shown as lace B, covering the tails from the heart design and stitch. This will be the dominant layer.

Once you have completed the heart design, the centre panel can be joined to the other five panels. There is an additional insertion of lace beading each side of the centre panel. Attach the beading to the insertion, leaving

2.5cm (1in) at the top and bottom. Join the beading to the insertion of the other panels, matching the bottom layer of insertion lace. The top of the skirt may need to be trimmed slightly to make it even.

Slash a 10cm (4in) opening in the centre back and sew a lace placket using the wider insertion lace. To do this, place a 25cm (10in) piece of lace to the V of the slash, right sides together, allowing 3mm (1/8in) of fabric to extend past the lace. Zigzag in place and trim fabric from behind lace. Fold the right-hand side of placket under and press. On the inside, stitch a dart in the lace at the bottom of the V.

Yoke: Lay the wider insertion lace around the outside edge of the yoke with the outside thread being on the edge of the fabric. Stitch and trim fabric from under lace.

Sleeve: Cut two strips of beading and four strips of the wider insertion lace 15cm (6in) long. Join a strip of the insertion either side of each strip of beading. Position each joined panel to the centre of each sleeve and zigzag in place.

Run gathering threads across the bottom of the sleeves and gather to 14cm (5 1/2in). Attach entredeux, beading and gathered lace edging. French seam the underarm seam.

Cut the armholes from the side front and back panels using the guide.

Join the sleeves to the skirt where indicated on pattern. Run two rows of gathering thread across the top of the skirt and the sleeve section, 6mm and 13mm (1/4in and 1/2in) from the edge.

Gather skirt and sleeve sections to fit yoke, fitting sleeve section between the small hearts. The bottom edge of the insertion lace should line up over the second row of gathering threads. Pin yoke to skirt and stitch with a short zigzag stitch wide enough to cover the heading threads and the gathering threads. Trim the extra fabric and lace ends away from behind the insertion lace.

Pull a heading thread from a length of edging lace and gather slightly to make a ruffle. Place heading of ruffle to bottom heading of yoke insertion lace. Zigzag together using a lighter stitch than you used to attach yoke. Extend the ruffle just beyond the centre backs, turn ends under and zigzag on the fold and trim.

To finish the neck edge, attach entredeux and a gathered lace edging, extending the trim slightly beyond centre backs. Fold ends under and zigzag on the fold. Trim excess fabric.

Pull heading threads in edging lace and attach to bottom lace insertion on skirt. Join ends with zigzag. You can gather the edging lace to the fullness you desire. Run ribbon through the beading on the sleeves, gather and tie a bow.

Attach two buttons to back yoke.

PETTICOAT

Cut six skirt panels, join with French seams and attach lace edging to the hem. Slash the centre back panel and sew a lace placket as for the dress. Cut out the armholes using the guide.

Zigzag a piece of the wider insertion lace to the bottom of the yoke. Fold centre backs on fold line and zigzag to neaten.

Position the fine edging lace to the neckline with the fancy edge of the lace to the cut edge of fabric, ends extending just beyond centre back. Zigzag in place, fold centre back ends under and zigzag on fold. Trim excess fabric from behind lace.

Finish armholes in skirt section the same as for the neckline.

Gather the top of skirt to fit the yoke, matching armholes to small hearts on yoke. Lay the insertion lace of the yoke on the second row of gathering threads of the skirt as before and zigzag together. Trim extra fabric from behind lace.

Finish with two buttons on centre back yoke.♥

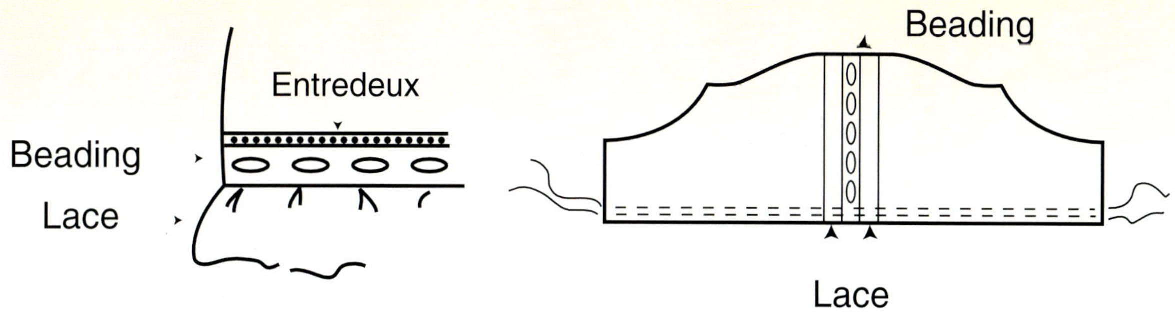

Garden Party

It's springtime again, the blossoms are out and it's time to enjoy the delights of a pretty garden. This charming floral dress with lace-trim, reflects the happy mood.

MATERIALS

- 50cm ($^1/_2$yd) floral fabric
- 50cm ($^1/_2$yd) fine gingham
- 40cm x 2.5cm ($^1/_2$yd x 1in) insertion lace
- 1m x 2.5cm (1$^1/_8$yd x 1in) cotton edging lace
- 30cm x 13mm ($^3/_8$yd x $^1/_2$in) elastic, for petticoat
- 5 x 6mm ($^1/_4$in) buttons
- Matching sewing thread
- Usual sewing requirements

To fit doll:
46cm (18in)
Finished length of dress:
32cm (12$^1/_2$in)

PREPARATION

Trace all pattern pieces from the pattern sheet and copy all markings. A 6mm ($^1/_4$in) seam allowance has been included in the pattern.

Cut two strips of fabric for the centre front button extensions 40.5cm x 5cm (16in x 2in). The skirt and slip are rectangles measuring 30.5cm x 114.3cm (12in x 45in).

DRESS

Join front and back bodice at shoulders using a small French seam. Gather top of sleeve with two rows of gathering stitch to fit bodice and stitch sleeve to bodice. Trim raw edges and neaten.

Gather bottom of sleeve to 14cm (5$^1/_2$in). Cut cuffs 5cm x 15.5cm (2in x 6in). Fold cuff in half lengthwise with wrong sides together and stitch to sleeve, right sides together. Trim and neaten. Set aside.

Join V-collar front and back sections at the shoulder, again using a small French seam, then zigzag gathered lace edging around outside edge. Sew gathered lace edging to the outside edge of sleeve caps, and gather raw edge to 5cm (2in). Centre sleeve cap under shoulder seam on

Garden Party

V-COLLAR DIAGRAM

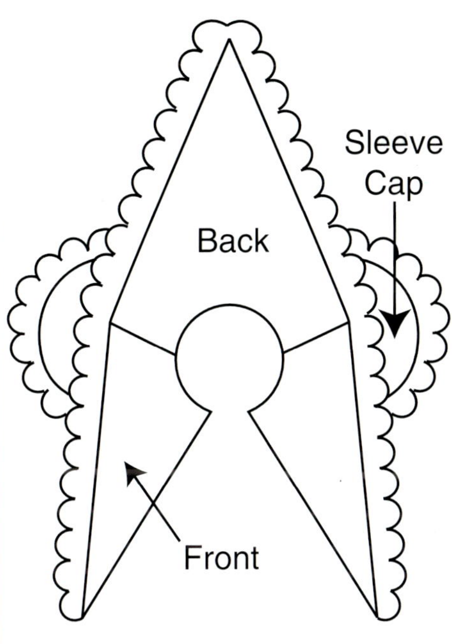

collar and zigzag to existing stitching line of lace, so that the join will be hidden under the lace of the collar. Pin collar to the bodice neckline, matching shoulder seams and raw edges. Set aside.

Join side and sleeve seams using a French seam. With right sides together, stitch beading to lower edge of bodice, sewing close to the edge of the beading. Trim to neaten.

Gather skirt with two rows of stitching to fit bodice. With right sides together, stitch close to the lower edge of beading. Trim to neaten.

Attach the button extension piece to wrong side of centre front bodice and skirt, press and turn to the right side. Fold under raw edge leaving a 1.3cm (1/2in) extension and top stitch in place. Stitch again on the fold to give it a sharp edge.

Fold under a 7.6cm (3in) hem on skirt and stitch.

Cut a bias strip 3.8cm x 30.5cm (1 1/2in x 12in). Fold in half lengthwise, pin and stitch to neckline over collar with right sides together and matching raw edges. Trim edges. Fold in half, then fold in the ends and hand sew the facing to the inside of the neckline.

Finish the dress with tiny buttons and buttonholes down the front.

HALF SLIP

Narrow hem top edge of slip, then fold under a 1.9cm (3/4in) casing for elastic. Stitch close to the edge. Run a 29cm x 13mm (11 1/2 x 1/2in) piece of elastic through casing and secure ends. Stitch down in several places to prevent elastic from rolling. Fold and stitch a 7.6cm (3in) hem. Stitch centre back seam and neaten edges.♥

Girl's Night Out

Winter can sometimes seem bleak but a wonderful way for a girl to brighten things up is to throw a slumber party. Pillow fights and chatter about boys are the order of the day, and of course some pretty new shortie pyjamas will be greatly appreciated.

MATERIALS

- 50cm (1/2yd) lightweight lingerie fabric
- 3m x 2.5cm (3 1/4yd x 1in) cotton edging lace
- 25cm (1/4yd) entredeux
- 60cm x 3mm (5/8yd x 1/8in) elastic
- 25cm x 6mm (10in x 1/4in) elastic
- Four x 4mm (1/4in) buttons
- Matching sewing threads
- Usual sewing requirements including duckbill scissors

To fit doll:
40.5cm (16in)
Finished length of top:
18.5cm (7 1/2in)

PREPARATION

Trace the pattern from the pattern sheet transferring all markings. A 6mm (1/4in) seam allowance has been included.

PYJAMA TOP

Fold under the centre front panels on the fold lines and press. Join the other five panels to fronts with a small French seam. There will be three panels across the back and one and a half panels for each front. Cut out the armhole curve at the top of the front and back side panels as indicated on pattern using the armhole guide. Refer to Diagram 1.

Position the lace edging so that the fancy edge is in line with the scalloped bottom edge of the pyjama top. Zigzag in place and trim away excess fabric carefully from behind the lace using the duckbill scissors.

In the same way as before, stitch lace edging onto the bottom of sleeves. Position the narrow elastic as indicated on the pattern and zigzag over the elastic using a wide stitch to form a casing. Draw up to a width of 12cm, secure ends of elastic and trim. Stitch sleeve seam.

Attach the underarm curve of the sleeve to the armhole of the side panels which you have cut out.

Fold centre fronts of yoke under on fold lines and press. Gather panelled section and top of sleeve to fit yoke. Refer to Diagram 2. Stitch with right sides together. NOTE: Unfold the centre fronts of yoke and panelled section to stitch, then fold under again and press.

Attach entredeux and gathered lace edging to neckline, extending 1cm (3/8in) past centre front edges. Fold ends to the inside, zigzag on the fold and trim.

Finish the top with buttons down the front.

Diagram 1

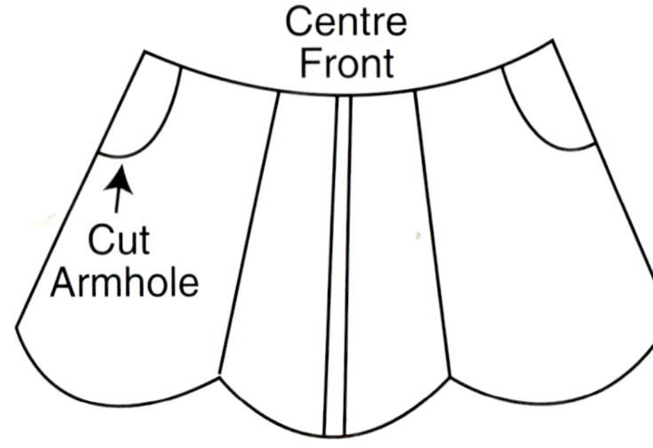

Diagram 2

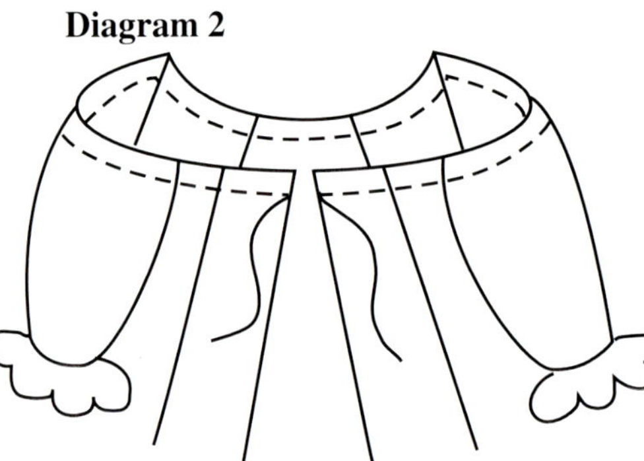

PYJAMA BOTTOMS

Stitch centre back seam. Narrow hem the top edge and fold under a 1.5cm (1/2in) casing. Run a 28cm (11in) piece of elastic through the casing and secure ends.

Attach edging lace to bottom of legs as for the sleeves. Zigzag elastic to bottom of leg as indicated on pattern, following instructions used for the sleeves. Draw up elastic to a measurement of 15cm (6in), secure ends and trim elastic.

Stitch centre front seam, then the inside leg seam, matching the crotch seams.♥

Below: Bottom of sleeve is drawn in by elastic to form a frill.

Dreaming of a White Christmas

Don't we all dream of having a white Christmas with log fires and mistletoe, maybe just once. This exquisite dress and cape make the perfect Christmas ensemble for a very special and memorable day.

Dreaming of a White Christmas

MATERIALS

DRESS AND PETTICOAT
- 60cm (5/8yd) lightweight cotton fabric
- 60cm (5/8yd) fine entredeux
- 7m x 40mm (7 5/8yd x 1 1/2in) cotton edging lace
- 1m x 1.9cm (1 1/8yd x 3/4in) cotton edging lace
- Three small buttons
- 1m x 6mm (1 1/8yd x 1/4in) blue double-sided satin ribbon
- 3m x 4mm (3 1/4yd x 1/8in) silk ribbon in three shades of pink
- 4m x 4mm (4 3/8yd x 1/8in) silk ribbon in pale green
- Three small buttons
- One tiny button or press stud for petticoat
- Matching sewing threads
- Assortment of tiny seed beads
- Usual sewing requirements including duckbill scissors
- Needle for embroidery

CAPE AND CAPELET
- 60cm (5/8yd) Vyella
- 40cm (1/2yd) lightweight lining fabric
- 30cm (12in) fine entredeux
- 60cm x 2.5cm wide (24in x 1in) cotton edging lace
- 1.2m x 2.5cm (1 1/4yd x 1in) double-sided satin ribbon for capelet ties
- 1.2m (1 1/4yd) store-bought satin trim (optional)
- 1 x 12mm button
- 1m x 6mm (1 1/8yd x 1/4in) blue double-sided satin ribbon
- 4m x 4mm (4 3/8yd x 1/8 in) silk ribbon in three shades of pink
- 3m x 4mm (3 1/4yd x 1/8 in) silk ribbon in pale green
- 1 skein each of green, light pink and medium-pink embroidery cotton
- Matching sewing threads
- Assortment of tiny seed beads
- Usual sewing requirements including duckbill scissors
- Needle for embroidery

To fit doll:
46cm (18in)

Finished length of dress:
32cm (12 1/2in)

PREPARATION
Trace pattern pieces from the pattern sheet, transferring all relevant markings. Read the instructions before cutting your fabric and note that a 6mm (1/4in) seam allowance has been included.

DRESS
Bodice: Cut two back bodices and one front bodice. Note that the back bodice is cut on the fold and will be a double layer but is treated as one layer. Sew the shoulder seams and set aside.

Working on the sleeves next, fold on the fold line, right sides together, and sew 2.5cm (1in) from the fold as indicated on the pattern. Press on the wrong side, flattening out to make a box pleat. Embellish the right side of the sleeve with a small feather

stitch, using green embroidery cotton. Add French knots at the ends of these stitches using shades of pink silk ribbon. Finish off with a silk spider's web rose with three French knots grouped together to make a bud and a scattering of light green lazy daisy and ribbon stitch leaves. Finally stitch single seed beads amongst the embroidery. Make sure that you leave at least 1.3 cm (1/2in) for the seam allowance at the bottom of the sleeve edge. Repeat for the other sleeve.

Once embellished, gather the bottom of the sleeve to a finished width of 12.7cm (5in). Add a band of entredeux and the narrow lace edging, slightly gathered. Gather the top of the sleeve with two rows of stitching to fit bodice measurement and stitch to bodice. Neaten seam edges.

With right sides together, stitch side bodice and sleeve seam. Turn, press and set aside.

Finish off the neck edge with entredeux and a gathered narrow lace edging. Extend the lace and entredeux 2.5 cm (1in) past each neck edge, fold under and zigzag on the fold. Trim extra lace from the wrong side.

Waistband: With the right sides together, stitch the ends of the two waistband pieces, turn and press. Attach the waistband to the lower bodice edge and then neaten the seam.

Now is the time to embellish the centre of the waistband if you wish. Tie a satin ribbon bow, using the 6mm (1/4in) wide, double-sided satin ribbon and either machine or hand stitch down in the middle of the band.

It helps to press the bow down before you try to stitch. Add a few silk ribbon spider's web roses and French knots across the front of the bow, then set aside.

NOTE: Stitch the embellishment only through the top layer of the waistband to hide the raw ends.

Skirt: Note how the back ends of the skirt are curved up and the front top edge is curved down in the centre of the skirt to fit the front waistband. Slightly gather the wider lace edging around the bottom edges of the skirt. The fancy edge of the lace should be even with the cut raw edge of the fabric. Stitch, then trim away extra fabric from behind lace.

Gather the top edge of the skirt to fit the lower edge of the waistband and position so that the lace overlaps at the back of the skirt. Stitch with right sides together. Neaten edges.

Add three small buttons and buttonholes down the centre back.

PETTICOAT

Cut a piece of fabric 33cm x 7.6cm (13in x 3in) for the waistband. Starting with the back skirt, slightly gather the wider lace edging and position it on the bottom of the petticoat with the fancy edge of the lace even with the lower edge of the fabric. Stitch, then trim extra fabric from under the lace.

Now do the next tier. Position the next layer of lace so the fancy edge of the lace barely tips the top of the previous row of lace. Do the remaining tiers of the petticoat in the same way, filling in the back skirt as indicated on the pattern. Stop about 2.5cm (1in) from the top edge of the waistline. Set aside.

For the petticoat front, stitch lace across the bottom edge of the skirt panel, following the instructions for the back. Trim extra fabric from under the lace edging.

With right sides together, stitch the side seams. Cut down 7.5cm (3in) from top at centre back to make a placket. With right sides together, position the narrow lace edging so that the fancy edge of lace is even with cut edge of fabric and stitch. Then stitch a dart in lace at the bottom of the V. Trim extra fabric from behind lace. Fold waistband in half lengthwise, right sides together and stitch the ends. Turn and press. With right sides and cut edges together, stitch waistband onto petticoat. One end will lap over the other. Finish off with either a tiny button or press stud.

CAPE AND CAPELET

Make sure you have transferred all the markings from the pattern as these will be very important.

Starting with the centre back, join the side back pieces of the cape to either side with right sides together. Press seams open.

Next, join the side front pieces to the centre fronts. Note the position of the little heart marks because that is where you will open the seam up for the armholes. Press seams open and set aside.

Repeat the same directions for the lining.

To join cape and lining, pin the two pieces, right sides together and stitch down the front, across the bottom and up the other front. Turn and press. Now open up the armholes and hand-whip the openings together with a tiny stitch.

Finish off the neck edge with entredeux and the narrow gathered lace edging, extending the lace 2.5cm (1in) over the fronts. Fold edges evenly with the fabric, then zigzag on the fold. Trim extra lace. Finish off with a small button at the top of the neck edge.

Now for the capelet. This is the time to show your creative flair. With right sides together, stitch the shoulder seams of both garment and lining. Press seams open, then set the lining aside.

Transfer the heart motif shown on the pattern sheet onto the centre of the capelet back. Embroider a small feather stitch with green embroidery cotton around the heart. Begin each side at the top curves of the heart so that the stitching will be going in the same direction on each side.

Tie another ribbon bow as you did for the waistband and attach at the top of the heart, following the same procedures you used on the waistband for the dress.

Using embroidery cotton and silk ribbon, embellish the heart and bow with a combination of French knot and bullion stitch flowers with lazy daisy and ribbon stitch leaves. Use several shades of pink silk ribbon for the spider's web roses at the top and lower edge. Decorate the fronts with small feather stitches in the corners topped with matching flowers, French knots and leaves. Finally add single seed beads amongst the embroidered design.

To join garment and lining, place both pieces right sides together and stitch around the edge, leaving a small opening at the bottom edge to turn through. Turn, press and hand stitch the opening closed.

Add double-sided silk ribbon ties at the neck edge and embellish the outside edge with a purchased fancy ribbon trim if desired.

The ends of the ties can be tacked under the ribbon trim if used, otherwise they can be positioned between the layers of the cape while you are stitching them together.♥

DOLL PROJECT

Sweet Heart Tea

A good old-fashioned tea party is an occasion to dress up and remember your best manners. This black velvet dress (left) by Susan York with its delicate machine embroidery and pink sash, is perfectly suitable attire.

MATERIALS

- 50cm(20in) black velvet
- 25cm (10in) pink cotton voile for collar and sash
- 30cm (12in) netting for half-slip
- Tear-away fabric stabiliser
- Tracing paper
- Matching sewing thread
- Machine embroidery thread in shades of pink and green
- General sewing requirements

Finished length:
34cm (13½ in)

To fit doll:
45.5 cm (18in)

PREPARATION

Trace patterns from the pattern sheet, transferring all markings and noting that a 6mm (¼in) seam allowance is included. Read the instructions before cutting out your fabric.

EMBROIDERY INSTRUCTIONS

The embroidery is done entirely by machine. It is reverse bobbin work. A heavier thread is wrapped on the bobbin and the tension on the bobbin case is loosened to accommodate the thread. Use a monofilament thread on top and tighten your machine top tension.

Some suggestions for types of thread suitable for the bobbin are DMC Perlé cotton No5, YLI Pearl Crown Rayon which is an overlocker thread, or ribbon floss. The design is sewn on the wrong side of the fabric so the bobbin will be sewing on the right side.

There are many stitches that can be used for this technique and you may like to experiment. On our garment a basic feather stitch was used on the vines of the keepsake heart motif, with a stitch length of 3.0 and width of 5.0 to 5.5.

Several stitches were used for the little flowers, including a single pattern of a triple straight stitch and a single pattern of a cross stitch.

BODICE

Cut a piece of voile for the sash 7.5cm x 115cm (3in x 45in) and

narrow hem the long sides. Cut into two pieces, giving two 57cm (22 1/2in) long sashes. Run two rows of gathering thread across one end of each sash and gather to approximately 1.3cm (1/2in). Position the sashes where indicated on the side front bodice pieces. With right sides together, position the centre front bodice over the side front pieces and stitch together, then neaten the seam.

To give the ends of the sash a finished pointed look, fold right sides together. Stitch across the ends, trim edges, then turn and press flat.

With front and back bodice pieces right sides together, stitch and neaten shoulder seams. Set aside.

SKIRT

Cut a piece of velvet 30.5cm x 115cm (12in x 45in) for the skirt which includes a 6.5cm (2 1/2in) hem. Trim the top of the skirt at centre front using the skirt guide.

Turn up the hem and press. Transfer the motif to the inside of the hem, using tracing paper. Draw seven pattern repeats, starting with a half scallop and ending with a half scallop. If there is some fabric left over it can be trimmed away.

Embroider the motif following the previous instructions.

Stitch and neaten the centre back seam, then slash seam 7.5cm (3in) from the top for a placket opening. Make the placket using insertion lace or bias fabric. Cut a piece of lace 20.5cm (8in) long. With right side out, pull dress opening to form a V, place the lace to the V, allowing 3mm (1/8in) of the fabric to extend past the lace. Stitch the lace to the fabric using a small zigzag, pivoting at the bottom of the V. Trim excess fabric from beneath the lace. Fold and press one side of the lace to the inside of the opening, then stitch a dart in the lace at the bottom of the V, using a small zigzag stitch.

Run two rows of gathering thread across the top of the skirt and gather to fit the bodice.

SLEEVES

Transfer the motif to the wrong side of the sleeves and embroider as for the skirt. Run tow rows of gathering thread across the top of the sleeve, one 6mm (1/4in) and one 1.3cm (1/2in) from the edge. Gather to fit the armhole of the bodice and stitch with right sides together, then remove gathering threads. Trim and neaten the seam.

Run two rows of gathering thread across the lower sleeve and gather to 14cm (5 1/2in). Cut a cuff piece from voile 5cm x 14cm (2in x 5 1/2in), fold in half lengthwise, wrong sides together. Pin to the wrong side of the sleeve bottom, with raw edges together, then stitch. Trim and neaten seam and press cuff flat.

With front and back bodice right sides together, stitch the sleeve and side seams in one line. Trim and neaten the seam and press towards the back. Fold up the sleeve cuff and press.

Matching centre fronts and with right sides together, stitch the skirt to the bodice and neaten seam.

COLLAR

Face top collar with a layer of tear away stabiliser and trace the motif onto the stabiliser. Embroider as before on the wrong side. Tear away the stabiliser. Place collar pieces right sides together and stitch around the outside edge. Clip corners, turn and press.

Pin the collar to the neck edge. Cut a 23cm x 3.8cm (9in x 1 1/2in) piece of voile on the bias for facing. Fold in half and press. Position facing around neck edge, lining up raw edges, then stitch, extending facing 2.5cm (1in) at centre backs. Zigzag raw edges together, fold facing to inside, turn in ends and tack down using a shell stitch. This gives the neck edge a scalloped look.

Finish the back bodice with three small fancy buttons.

HALF SLIP

Fold the netting in half lengthwise and stitch a 1.3cm (1/2in) casing. Run a 28cm (11in) piece of elastic through the casing and secure at each end. With right sides together, stitch centre back seam. ♥

Heirlooms of Tomorrow

In terms of today's serious doll collector, American Susan York has a somewhat unconventional collection of dolls. There are no Jumeaus, Brus, Kestners or character children, no china-heads or wide-eyed moderns, in fact Susan's collection consists entirely of 16½ to 18 inch vinyl dolls.

TEXT BY KIRSTY HOLMES

But this doesn't make them any less special, in fact Susan takes them everywhere she goes because they are the perfect models for the exquisite doll garments she designs and teaches.

"I'm an heirloom sewing designer and I used to design children's clothes. But I have three boys and it seemed futile to keep making all of the big dresses when there was nobody around to wear them or appreciate them," Susan explains. "I consider myself more of a technique teacher and I really don't care what my students make as long as I'm able to teach and portray a technique. So the doll garments seemed to be the perfect avenue for that, because they are much smaller, easier to complete and less expensive."

"Many serious doll collectors think it is almost a sin that I invest so much time and money into these types of dresses for this type of doll," she admits. "But I think of it as an in-between kind of doll. It is a doll for children to play with and they learn to handle this doll so when they do get older, they are able to appreciate the finer pieces of porcelain and the finer collectable dolls."

So why the vinyl dolls? "I've been doing heirloom sewing since about 1978 and I started a children's line of patterns. Many of the women that had made my children's patterns had daughters who owned these All American Girl vinyl dolls, and they wanted matching doll outfits." So, as a special favour, Susan drafted a doll pattern to match the original child pattern and was overwhelmed by its popularity. Consequently, she decided to focus her efforts more on these small-scale success stories, and has been doing so for four years.

What makes this particular type of doll even more appealing to Susan is the fact that it is readily available and relatively inexpensive. "I probably have about 20 dolls, they are not all the American Girl doll, but similar and they are available at a variety of places such as the local discount store or a department store," she says. "This way, people can also shop for a doll within their budget -$15 to $100- it depends on what they want to spend. There are a lot of dolls in that size, and my patterns will fit dolls from about 16½ inches to 20 inches tall."

Susan's garments incorporate a delicious combination of delicate embroidery, smocking, ribbons and laces with the most exquisite fabrics, resulting in stunning garments to be treasured and admired for many years to come. In effect, she really is creating the heirlooms of tomorrow.

"I think of heirloom as that Victorian, early 1900s, fantasy kind of look, something our great grandmothers might have worn," she smiles. "Heirloom sewing is not really a technique per se, it is more to do with the fabrics and supplies you use – the finer laces and trims and ribbons. It is a delicate kind of art."

Not everything Susan makes is heirloom, she has "fun" outfits as well. "I try to introduce a different sewing technique every month, it is still in the heirloom field, but not all frills and Edwardian looking." If her students really love a particular technique or look they have an opportunity to take a more intensive class and transpose what they have learnt into a bigger project.

Travelling continuously around America to teach, Susan has built up a healthy reputation amongst her many sewing groups and her mail order service is becoming increasingly popular as the word spreads. Back home, she has a group of about 50 people from within a 20 mile radius of Nashville that meet once a month to "play the game" with her.

Susan also runs a pattern club (which she calls a doll club) where she distributes a different pattern each month. "All of my

patterns are a story, they are not just instructions to sew the seams and put a button hole in, I actually write a story. For example, last January I called the pattern Girls' Night Out and I told a story of how all the girls (dolls) got together for a slumber party, they all had their pyjamas and sleeping bags, they talked about boys and did each others' hair, all that kind of fantasy stuff." she explains.

"Every month last year involved a pattern of that nature. This year, we are having a different tea party each month. The girls get together and wear little lace gloves and pour tea.

"I find that the women who sew also like the fantasy part. They can go back and play little girl and escape from everyday life. It's cheaper than therapy," she laughs.

Because Susan is in transit so often, her dolls are usually kept packed away in suitcases, ready for the next adventure.

"I keep the girls all dressed up and with their toys and we live in the car a lot," she says. "I have different sets of girls for different occasions."

The car is also probably the safest place for the dolls to be – a house with three young boys living in it is has no room for dolls. "Unfortunately I can't display the dolls around the house, I wish I could but I'm having to step over baseball bats, football helmets and there just isn't room for my dolls."

Realising the 'sacrifice' their mother is making by keeping the dolls packed away, Susan's sons offer much support towards her enterprise. "My sons are very supportive, they help load and unload the car and they go to shows with me and are very entertaining."

Even so, she has met a little bit of jealousy from her young teenage son because he feels Samantha gets more new "fun things" than he does.

"Samantha is the main doll in the collection and we talk about her as if she were a sister," Susan explains. "We are always looking for toys and things that Samantha might like to do. My husband just bought a motorcycle and so I decided that Samantha just has to have a motorcycle outfit, to be a motorcycle babe."

While there may be a smidgin of jealousy, Susan points out that her sons are smart enough to realise that Samantha makes money and that money supports their hobbies, so they understand.

Susan shows her gratitude for their support by attending and vocally supporting the boys at their respective sports. "They play baseball and football and soccer and so I follow them around and I'm also the loudest cheerleader. That just about takes up the rest of my time."

Contemplating her future, Susan admits she would love to venture out to other countries but it is a matter of making the contacts and finding a market. In 1993 and 1994 she did get the chance to visit Australia as a teacher with the Martha Pullen School, and she hopes to visit our shores again in the future. There is no doubt she would receive a warm welcome on her return.

"I travel a lot and I enjoy it, but I try to limit the time because my children are not going to be young forever," she says. "Right now I'm a fun date for them but pretty soon I won't be a fun date and then I'll have the rest of my life to really travel hard." ♥

Adjusting the Patterns

In this collection, each pattern is designed for a doll of a specific height, but before commencing to sew, you should measure your doll and check those measurements against the pattern.

Dolls of the same height may differ in their body measurements, so by testing the fitting of pattern parts before cutting out, adjustments can be made.

All patterns are given full size and include seam allowances and an additional allowance for ease of slipping the garment on the doll. Unlike real-life dressmaking, dolls are usually inflexible and the garment itself must have enough room for the doll without tearing or breaking the stitches. You need to ensure that the neck of the dress is big enough to pass over the doll's head, the sleeves over the hands and the feet through the legs of her pants.

You may like to prepare a preliminary muslin (or toile) of the garment, fit it on the doll and make any necessary adjustments before cutting your 'real' garment. First trace the patterns on to tissue paper or Vilene and mark all your alterations on the tracing, then cut out the pattern pieces around the new outline. Pin the pieces on to the doll to check the fit, and if necessary, alter the marking. Then use the adjusted pattern pieces to cut your muslin or toile, before cutting into valuable and sometimes scarce material.♥

Always measure your doll and then adjust the pattern to suit - you can make a trial dress from the muslin and then adjust from the fitting.
For the bodice fit, measure:

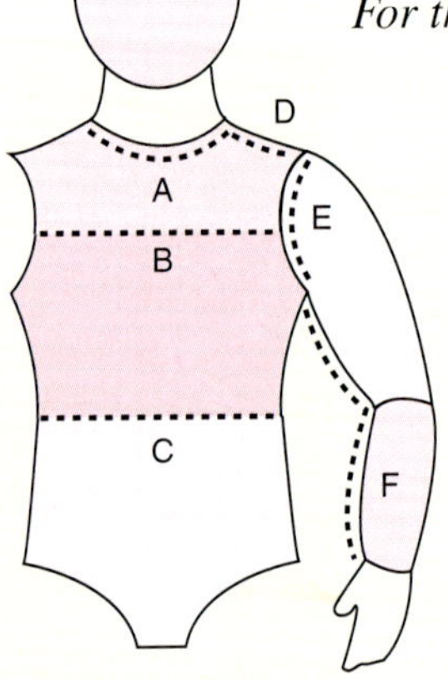

A neck
B chest
C waist
D shoulder
E armhole
F sleeve length from wrist to armhole base.

HELPFUL HINT

If you find the measuring difficult, use a string or cotton tape, then transfer to a tape measure.